I RISE IN FLAME, CRIED THE PHOENIX

BY TENNESSEE WILLIAMS

The action of this play, which is imaginary, takes place in the French Riviera where D. H. Lawrence died.

Not long before Lawrence's death an exhibition was held of his paintings in London. Primitive in technique and boldly sensual in matter, this exhibition created a little tempest. The pictures were seized by the police and would have been burned if the authorities had not been restrained by an injunction. At this time Lawrence's great study of sexual passion, *Lady Chatterly's Lover*, was likewise under the censor's ban, as much of his work had been in the past.

Lawrence felt the mystery and power of sex, as the primal life urge, and was the life-long adversary of those who wanted to keep the subject locked away in the cellars of prudery. Much of his work is chaotic and distorted by tangent obsessions, such as his insistence upon the woman's subservience to the male, but all in all his work is probably the greatest modern monument to the dark roots of creation.

T. W.
New Orleans, September, 1941.

CHARACTERS

Lawrence

Frieda

Bertha [Brett]

I Rise In Flame, Cried The Phoenix

The scene of the play is at Vence in the Alpes Maritimes.

It is late afternoon.

LAWRENCE *is seated on the sun-porch, the right wall of which is a window that faces the sun. A door in this wall opens out on the high sea-cliff. It is windy: the surf can be heard.* LAWRENCE *looks out that way. Behind him, on the left wall, woven in silver and scarlet and gold, is a large silk banner that bears the design of the Phoenix in a nest of flames—*LAWRENCE'S *favorite symbol. He sits quite still. His beard is fiercely red and his face is immobile, the color of baked clay with tints of purple in it. The hands that gripped the terrible stuff of life and made it plastic are folded on the black-and-white checked surface of an invalid's blanket. The long fingers of the Welsh coal-miners, with their fine blond hairs and their knobby knuckles, made for rending the black heart out of the earth, are knotted together with a tightness that betrays the inner lack of repose. His slightly distended nostrils draw the breath in and out as tenderly as if it were an invisible silk thread that any unusual tension might snap in two. Born for contention, he is contending with something he can't get his hands on. He has to control his fury. And so he is seated motionless in the sunlight—wrapped in a checkered blanket and lavender wool shawl.—The tiger in him is trapped but not destroyed yet.*

FRIEDA *comes in, a large handsome woman of fifty, rather like a Valkyrie. She holds up a fancily wrapped little package.*

LAWRENCE. (*Without even turning his head.*) —What is it?

FRIEDA. Something left on the doorstep.

LAWRENCE. Give it here.

FRIEDA. The donor is anonymous.

I only caught a glimpse of her through the window.

LAWRENCE. A woman?

FRIEDA. Yes . . .

LAWRENCE. Yes . . .

FRIEDA. Some breathless little spinster in a blue pea-jacket.
She stuck it on the porch and scuttled back down the hill before
I could answer the doorbell.

LAWRENCE. (*His voice rising querulously shrill.*) It's for me,
isn't it?

FRIEDA. Ja, it's for you.

(*In German.*)

LAWRENCE. Well, give it here, damn you, you ——!

FRIEDA. *Tch!*

I thought that the sun had put you in a good humor.

LAWRENCE. It's put me in a vile humor.

We've sat here making faces at each other the whole afternoon.

I say to the sun, Make me well, you old bitch, give me strength,
take hold of my hands and pull me up out of this chair!

But the sun is a stingy *haus-frau.* She goes about sweeping the
steps and pretends not to hear me begging.

Ah, well, I don't blame her. I never did care for beggars myself
very much.

A man shouldn't beg. A man should seize what he wants and tear
it out of the hands of the adversary. And if he can't get it, if he
can't tear it away, then he should let it go and give up and be con-
tented with nothing.

Look.

(*He has unwrapped package.*)

A little jar of orange marmalade.

(*Smiles with childish pleasure.*)

This is the month of August put in a bottle.

FRIEDA. Ja! *Sehr gut.*

You can have it for breakfast.

LAWRENCE. (*Drawing tenderly on the fine gold thread.*) Uh-huh.

I can have it for breakfast as long as I live, huh, Frieda?

It's just the right size for that.

FRIEDA. Shut up.
(*Starts to take jar from him. Quick as a cat he snatches her wrist in a steel grip.*)
LAWRENCE. Leave go of it, damn you!
FRIEDA. (*Laughing.*) My God, but you still are strong!
LAWRENCE. You didn't think so?
FRIEDA. I had forgotten. You've been so gentle lately.
LAWRENCE. Thought you'd tamed me?
FRIEDA. Yes, but I should have known better.
I should have suspected what you've been doing inside you, lapping that yellow cream up, you sly old fox, sucking the fierce red sun in your body all day and turning it into venom to spew in my face!
LAWRENCE. No—I've been making a trap.
I've been making a shiny steel trap to catch you in, you vixen! Now break away if you can!
FRIEDA. (*Grinning and wincing.*) Oh, God, how you hurt!
LAWRENCE. (*Slowly releasing her.*) —Don't lie . . .
You with that great life in you—
Why did God give you so much and me so little?
You could take my arm and snap it like a dry stick.
FRIEDA. No.—You were always the stronger one.
Big as I am, I never could beat you, could I?
LAWRENCE. (*With satisfaction.*) No. You couldn't.
(*His breath rasps hoarsely.*)
Put the jar down on the sill.
FRIEDA. (*Complying.*) Ahh, there's a card stuck on it.
"From one of your devoted readers."
And on the other side it says—
"I worship you, Mr. Lawrence, because I know that only a god could know so much about Life!"
LAWRENCE. (*Dryly.*) In looking for God so unsuccessfully myself, it seems that I have accidentally managed to create one for an anonymous spinster in a blue pea-jacket.
Upon the altar of her pagan deity she places a dainty jar of orange marmalade!
What a *cynical* little woman she is!
Only the little ones of the earth, who scuttle downhill like pebbles dislodged by the rain, are really capable of such monumental disbelief.

They find their god and they give him marmalade.
If I find mine—ever—
If I found mine, I'd tear the heart out of my body and burn it before him.
FRIEDA. Your health is returning.
LAWRENCE. What makes you think so?
FRIEDA. You are getting so sentimental about yourself and so unappreciated and so misunderstood.—You can't stand Jesus Christ because he beat you to it. Oh, how you would have loved to suffer the *original* crucifixion!
LAWRENCE. If only I had your throat between my fingers.
FRIEDA. (*Crouching beside him.*) Here is my throat.—Now choke me.
LAWRENCE. (*Gently touching her throat with tips of his fingers.*) Frieda—do you think I will ever get back to New Mexico?
FRIEDA. You will do what you want to do, Lawrence. There has never been any kind of resistance you couldn't jump over or crawl under or squeeze through.
LAWRENCE. Do you think I will ever get back on a strong white horse and go off like the wind across the glittering desert?
I'm not a literary man, I'm tired of books.
Nobody knows what an ugly joke it is that a life like mine should only come out in books.
FRIEDA. What else should it come out in?
LAWRENCE. In some kind of violent action.
But all that I ever do is go packing around the world with women and manuscripts and a vile disposition.
I pretend to be waging a war with bourgeois conceptions of morality, with prudery, with intellectuality, with all kinds of external forces that aren't external at all. What I'm fighting with really's the little old maid in myself, the breathless little spinster who scuttles back down the hill before God can answer the doorbell.
Now I want to get back on the desert and try all over again to become a savage.
I want to stand up on the Lobos and watch a rainstorm coming ten miles off like a silver-helmeted legion of marching giants.
And that's what I'm going to do, damn you!
FRIEDA. Whoever said that you wouldn't?
LAWRENCE. You!—You know that I won't.

You know that the male savage part of me's dead and all that's left is the old pusillanimous squaw.

Women have such a fine intuition of death.

They smell it coming before it's started even.

I think it's women that actually let death in, they whisper and beckon and slip it the dark latch-key from under their aprons,—don't they?

FRIEDA. No.—It's women that pay the price of admission for life. And all of their lives they make of their arms a cross-bar at the door that death wants to come in by.

Men love death—Women don't.

Men cut wounds in each other and women stop the bleeding.

LAWRENCE. Yes. By drinking the blood.

Don't touch me so much!

(*Releasing his fingers.*)

Your fingers, they make me feel weaker, they drain the strength out of my body.

FRIEDA. Oh, no, no, no, they put it back *in*, mein liebchen.

LAWRENCE. I want you to promise me something.

If I should die, Frieda—the moment I'm dying, please to leave me alone!—Don't touch me, don't put your hands on me, and don't let anyone else.—I have a nightmarish feeling that while I'm dying I'll be surrounded by women.—They'll burst in the door and the windows the moment I lose the strength to push them away—They'll moan and they'll flutter like doves around the burnt-out Phoenix—They'll cover my face and my hands with filmy kisses and little trickling tears—Alma the nymphomaniac and the virginal Bertha—All of the under and over-sexed women I've known, who think me the oracle of their messed-up libidos—They'll all return with their suffocating devotion—I don't want that.—I want to die like a lonely old animal does, I want to die fiercely and cleanly with nothing but anger and fear and other hard things like that to deal with at the finish.

You understand, Frieda?

I've still got a bit of the male left in me and that's the part that I'm going to meet death with.

When the last bleeding comes, and it *will* in a little while now, I won't be put into bed and huddled over by women. I won't stay in the house, Frieda. I'll open this door and go outside on the cliff. And I don't wish to be followed. That's the important point,

Frieda. I'm going to do it alone. With the rocks and the water. Sunlight—starlight on me. No hands, no lips, no women!—Nothing but—pitiless nature ——
FRIEDA. I don't believe you. I don't think people want nothing but "pitiless nature" when they're ——
LAWRENCE. Frieda!
You mean you refuse?
FRIEDA. No. I consent absolutely.
LAWRENCE. You give me your promise?
FRIEDA. (*In German.*) Yes, a hundred times, yes!
Now think about something else.—I'll go fix tea.
(*Starts to go out.*)
LAWRENCE. (*Suddenly noticing something.*) Ahh, my God.
FRIEDA. What's the matter?
LAWRENCE. Put the aquarium on the window-sill.
FRIEDA. Why?
LAWRENCE. So I can keep an eye on it.—That detestable cat has attacked the goldfish again.
FRIEDA. How do you know?
LAWRENCE. How do I know? There used to be *four*, now there's *three! Beau Soleil!*
FRIEDA. She's gone outside.
LAWRENCE. To lick her chops, God damn her!
Set the goldfish bowl on the window-sill.
FRIEDA. You can't keep them there in the sun. The sun will kill them.
LAWRENCE. (*Furiously.*) Don't answer me back, put 'em *there!*
FRIEDA. (*In German.*) All right, all right!
(*Hastens to place aquarium on sill.*)
LAWRENCE. You know what I think? I think you *fed* her the fish. It's like you to do such a thing.
You're both so fat, so rapacious, so viciously healthy and hungry!
FRIEDA. Such a fuss over a goldfish!
LAWRENCE. It isn't just a goldfish.
FRIEDA. What is it then?
LAWRENCE. —Now that my strength's used up I can't help thinking how much of it's been thrown away in squabbling with you.
FRIEDA. (*Suddenly covering her face.*) Oh, Lawrence.
LAWRENCE. —What are you doing? Crying?

Stop it. I can't stand crying. It makes me worse.

FRIEDA. I think you *hate* me, Lawrence.

(*After a moment he shyly touches her arm.*)

LAWRENCE. —Don't believe me.—I love you.

Ich liebe dich, Frieda.

Put some rum in the tea.

I'm getting much stronger, so why should I feel so weak?

FRIEDA. (*Touching his forehead.*) I wish you would go back to bed.

LAWRENCE. The bed's an old tar-baby. I'd get stuck. How do I know that I'd get loose again?—Is my forehead hot?

(FRIEDA *places her hand tenderly over his eyes.*)

LAWRENCE. (*In a childish treble.*) "Lady-bug, lady-bug, fly away home, thine house is on fire, thy children will burn!"

(*Smiling slightly.*)

My mother used to sing that whenever she saw one.—Simple.— Most people are so damned complicated and yet there is nothing much to them.

FRIEDA. (*Starts out—pauses before banner.*) Ahh, you old Phoenix—You brave and angry old bird in your nest of flames!— I think you are just a little bit sentimental.

LAWRENCE. (*Leaning suddenly forward.*) Tea for three!

FRIEDA. Who is it?

LAWRENCE. Bertha!—Back from London with news of the exhibition.

(*Pulls himself out of chair.*)

FRIEDA. What are you doing?

LAWRENCE. I'm going outside to meet her.

FRIEDA. Sit down, you fool!—I'll meet her.

And don't you dare to ask her to stay in this house—If you do, I'll leave!

(*Goes out.*)

LAWRENCE. Cluck-cluck-cluck-cluck!—You think I'm anxious to have more hens around me?

(*He wriggles fretfully in chair for a moment. Then throws off blanket and pushes himself to his feet. Stumbling with dizziness and breathing heavily, he moves to inside rear door of porch. Reaches it, pauses with a fit of coughing. Looks anxiously back toward chair—*)

No, no, damn you—I *won't!*

(*Looks up at Phoenix. Straightens heroically and goes out. After a few moments* FRIEDA *returns with* BERTHA, *a small, sprightly person, an English gentlewoman with the quick voice and eyes of a child.*)

FRIEDA. My God, he's got up!

BERTHA. He shouldn't?

FRIEDA. Another hemorrhage will kill him. The least exertion is likely to bring one on.

Lorenzo, where are you?

LAWRENCE. (*From rear.*) Quit clucking, you old wet hen. I'm fetching the tea.

BERTHA. Go back to him, make him stop!

FRIEDA. He wouldn't.

BERTHA. Does he want to die?

FRIEDA. Oh, no, no, no!

He has no lungs and yet he goes on breathing.

The heart's worn out and yet the heart keeps beating.

It's awful to watch, this struggle, I wish he would stop, I wish that he'd give it up and just let go!

BERTHA. Frieda!

FRIEDA. His body's a house that's made out of tissue-paper and caught on fire. The walls are transparent, they're all lit up with the flame!

When people are dying the spirit ought to go out, it ought to die out slowly before the flesh, you shouldn't be able to see it so terribly brightly consuming the walls that give it a place to inhabit!

BERTHA. I never have believed that Lorenzo could die.

I don't think he will even now.

FRIEDA. But can he do it?

Live without body, I mean, be just a flame with nothing to feed itself on?

BERTHA. The Phoenix could do it.

FRIEDA. The Phoenix was legendary. Lorenzo's a man.

BERTHA. He's more than a man.

FRIEDA. I know you always thought so. But you're mistaken.

BERTHA. You'd never admit that Lorenzo was a god.

FRIEDA. Having slept with him—No, I wouldn't.

BERTHA. There's more to be known of a person than carnal knowledge.

FRIEDA. But carnal knowledge comes first.

BERTHA. I disagree with you.

FRIEDA. And also with Lawrence, then. He always insisted you couldn't know women until you had known their bodies.

BERTHA. Frieda, I think it is you who kept him so much in his body!

FRIEDA. Well, if I did he's got that to thank me for.

BERTHA. I'm not so sure it's something to be thankful for.

FRIEDA. What would you have done with him if ever you got your claws on him?

BERTHA. Claws?—Frieda!

FRIEDA. You would have plucked him out of his body.
Where would he be?—In the air?—
Ahhhh, your deep understanding and my stupidity always!

BERTHA. Frieda!

FRIEDA. You just don't know, the meaning of Lawrence escapes you!
In all his work he celebrates the body!
How he despises the prudery of people that want to hide it!

BERTHA. Oh, Frieda, the same old quarrel!

FRIEDA. Yes, let's stop it!
What's left of Lorenzo, let's not try to divide it!

BERTHA. What's left of Lorenzo is something that can't be divided!

FRIEDA. Shhh!—He's coming.

BERTHA. (*Advancing a few steps to door.*) *Lorenzo!*

LAWRENCE. (*Out of sight.*) "Pussy-cat, pussy-cat, where have you been?"

BERTHA. (*Gaily.*) "I've been to London to look at the queen!"

LAWRENCE. (*Clear.*) "Pussy-cat, pussy-cat, what did you do there?"

BERTHA. (*Her voice catching slightly.*) "I chased a little mouse—under a chair!"

(*Laughing,* HE *appears in doorway, pushing a small tea-cart.* BERTHA *stares aghast.*)

LAWRENCE. Yes, I know—I know. . . .
I look an amateur's job of embalming, don't I?

BERTHA. (*Bravely.*) Lorenzo, you look very well.

LAWRENCE. It isn't rouge, it's the fever!
I'm burning, burning, and still I never burn out.

The doctors are all astonished. And disappointed.
And as for that expectant widow of mine—She's almost given up hope.
BERTHA. (*Moves to assist him with table.*)
LAWRENCE. Don't bother me. I can manage.
FRIEDA. He won't be still, he won't rest.
LAWRENCE. Cluck-cluck-cluck-cluck!
You better watch out for the rooster, you old wet hen!
FRIEDA. A wonderful Chanticleer you make in that lavender shawl!
LAWRENCE. Who put it on me? *You*, you bitch!
(*Flings it off.*)
Rest was never any good for me, Brett.
BERTHA. Rest for a little while.
Then we go sailing again!
LAWRENCE. We three go sailing again!
"Rub-a-dub-dub!
Three fools in a tub!
The Brett, the Frieda,
the old Fire-eater!"
BERTHA. (*Tugging at his beard.*) The old Fire-eater!
LAWRENCE. Watch out!
Now I'll have to comb it.
(*Takes out a little mirror and comb.*)
FRIEDA. So vain of his awful red whiskers!
LAWRENCE. (*Combing.*) She envies my beard.
All women resent men's whiskers.
They can't stand anything, Brett, that distinguishes men from women.
FRIEDA. Quite the contrary.
(*Pours tea.*)
LAWRENCE. They take the male in their bodies—but only because they secretly hope that he won't be able to get back out again, that he'll be captured for good!
FRIEDA. What kind of talk for a maiden-lady to hear?!
LAWRENCE. There she goes again, Brett—obscene old creature!
Gloating over your celibacy!
FRIEDA. Gloating over it? Never!
I think how lucky she is that she doesn't have to be told a hundred times every day that man is life and that woman is just a passive hunk of protoplasm.

LAWRENCE. I never said passive. I always said malignant.
(*Puts comb away and stares in the mirror.*)
Ain't I the devil to look at?
FRIEDA. I tell you, Brett, his ideas of sex are becoming right down
cosmic! When the sun comes up in the morning—You know what
he says?
No, I won't repeat it!
And when the sun's going down—
Oh, well, you will hear him yourself.
LAWRENCE. (*Chuckling.*) Yes, I always make the same remark.
You'll hear me yourself in just a few more minutes . . .
(*Puts mirror away.*)
Well, Brett!
BERTHA. Well, Lorenzo?
LAWRENCE. You haven't said anything yet.
BERTHA. Anything? About what?
LAWRENCE. What do you think that I sent you to London for?
BERTHA. To get me out of the way!
LAWRENCE. What else?
Out with it, damn you! The show!
How did they like my pictures?
BERTHA. Well ——
FRIEDA. Go on, Brett, tell him the truth. The monster will not
be satisfied till he hears it!
BERTHA. Well ——
FRIEDA. The exhibition was a complete fiasco!
Just as I said it would be!
LAWRENCE. You mean that they *liked* my dairies?
FRIEDA. *Liked* your pictures?
They called your pictures *disgusting!*
LAWRENCE. Ah!—*Success!*
They said that I couldn't paint?
That I draw like a child?
They called my figures grotesque? Lumpy, obscene, misshapen,
monstrous, deformed?
BERTHA. You must have seen the reviews, you've read them your-
self!
LAWRENCE. Why? Am I quoting exactly?
FRIEDA. Yes, you are quoting exactly!

LAWRENCE. And what did the public think? And what of the people?
FRIEDA. The people laughed!
LAWRENCE. They laughed?
FRIEDA. Of course they laughed!
Lorenzo, you're not a painter, you're a writer!
Why, you can't even draw a straight line!
LAWRENCE. No! But I can draw a *crooked* line, Frieda.
And that is the reason that I can put *life* in my pictures!
How was the attendance? How many came to look?
BERTHA. After the disturbance, the entrance had to be roped off to hold back the crowds.
LAWRENCE. Disturbance? What disturbance?
FRIEDA. Just look. The monster's exulting!
LAWRENCE. Go on, tell me what happened!
BERTHA. A group of ladies' club members attempted to slash the picture of Adam and Eve.
(LAWRENCE *shakes with laughter.*)
FRIEDA. Lorenzo! Stop that!
BERTHA. That was what called the attention of the police.
LAWRENCE. The police?
(*He rises.*)
What did they do to my pictures? Burn them? DESTROY THEM?
BERTHA. No. We got out an injunction to keep them from burning the pictures.
LAWRENCE. The pictures are safe?
BERTHA. The pictures are safe, Lorenzo.
FRIEDA. Sit down in that chair or I'll have to put you to bed!
(*Tries to push him down.* HE *slaps her fiercely.*)
BERTHA. Lorenzo!
LAWRENCE. Vaunting her power, gloating over my weakness!
Put me to bed? Just try it—I dare you to touch me!
FRIEDA. Lawrence, sit down in the chair or you'll start the bleeding again.
(HE *stares at her for a moment, then obeys slowly.*)
LAWRENCE. (*Weakly.*) Give me back that shawl.
The sun's getting weaker.
The young blond god is beginning to be seduced by the harlot of darkness . . .

FRIEDA. Now he's going to make his classic remarks on the sunset.

(*She puts shawl about him.*)

LAWRENCE. Yes—the pictures—they weren't very good but they had a fierce life in them.

BERTHA. They had *you* in them. But why did you want to *paint*, Lawrence?

LAWRENCE. Why did I want to *write*?

Because I'm an artist.—What is an artist?—A man who loves life too intensely, a man who loves life till he hates her and has to strike out with his fist like I struck at Frieda ——

To show her he knows her tricks, and he's still the master!

(*The smoky yellow light is beginning to dim.*)

Oh, Brett, oh, Frieda ——

I wanted to stretch out the long, sweet arms of my art and embrace the whole world!

But it isn't enough to go out to the world with love.

The world's a woman you've got to take by storm.

And so I doubled my fist and I struck and I struck.

Words weren't enough—I had to have color, too.

I took to paint and I painted the way that I wrote!

Fiercely, without any shame!

This is life, I told them, life is like *this!*

Wonderful! Dark! Terrific!

They banned my books and they wanted to burn my pictures!

That's how it is—When first you look at the sun it strikes you blind—Life's—blinding. . . .

(*Stirs and leans forward.*)

The sun's—going down.

He's seduced by the harlot of darkness.

FRIEDA. Now he is going to say it—Stop up your ears!

LAWRENCE. Now she has got him, they're copulating together! The sun is exhausted, the harlot has taken his strength and now she will start to destroy him. She's eating him up. . . .

Oh, but he won't stay down. He'll climb back out of her belly and there will be light.

In the end there will always be light—And I am the prophet of it!

(*He rises with difficulty.*)

BERTHA. Lorenzo!

FRIEDA. Lawrence, be careful!

LAWRENCE. Shut up! Don't touch me!

(*He staggers to the great window.*)

In the end there is going to be light—Light, light!

(*His voice rises and he stretches his arms out like a Biblical prophet.*)

Great light!—Great, blinding, universal *light!*

And *I*—I'm the *Prophet* of it!

(*Staggers and clutches his mouth.*)

FRIEDA. *Lawrence!*

BERTHA. (*Terrified.*) What *is* it?

FRIEDA. The *bleeding!*

BERTHA. *Lorenzo!*

(*She would rush to him but* FRIEDA *clutches her arm.*)

LAWRENCE. Don't touch me, you women.

I want to do it alone.—Don't move till it's finished.

(*Gradually, as though forced down to the earth by invisible arms, he begins to collapse—his hands clutch onto the curtains—his knees collapse.*)

BERTHA. (*Struggling fiercely with* FRIEDA.) Let me go, let me go, I want to go to him!

FRIEDA. Not yet—not yet—one moment!

(*His fingers let go. He slides to the floor. He is lifeless.*)

FRIEDA. (*Releasing the other woman.*) Now.—Go to him.—It's finished.

(*She covers her face.* BERTHA *rushes moaning to* LAWRENCE *and crouches beside him.*)

(*The sun disappears.*)

SLOW CURTAIN

PROPERTY LIST

Silk banner—phoenix in nest of flames
Checkered blanket
Lavender wool shawl
Fancily wrapt little package
Jar of marmalade
Bowl of goldfish in aquarium
Small tea-cart with tea things
Small mirror and comb

NOTES
(Use this space to make notes for your production)

www.ingramcontent.com/pod-product-compliance
Lightning Source LLC
Chambersburg PA
CBHW071637030726
47592CB00005B/1880